Terms and Conditions

LEGAL NOTICE

The Publisher has strived to be as accurate and complete as possible in the creation of this report, notwithstanding the fact that he does not warrant or represent at any time that the contents within are accurate due to the rapidly changing nature of the Internet.

While all attempts have been made to verify information provided in this publication, the Publisher assumes no responsibility for errors, omissions, or contrary interpretation of the subject matter herein. Any perceived slights of specific persons, peoples, or organizations are unintentional.

In practical advice books, like anything else in life, there are no guarantees of income made. Readers are cautioned to reply on their own judgment about their individual circumstances to act accordingly.

This book is not intended for use as a source of legal, business, accounting or financial advice. All readers are advised to seek services of competent professionals in legal, business, accounting and finance fields.

You are encouraged to print this book for easy reading.

Table Of Contents

Forward

Chapter 1: Beginning With Content

Chapter 2: Auction Sites

Chapter 3:
Transcription and Translation

Chapter 4:
Writing e-Books

Chapter 5:
Search Engine Optimization

Chapter 6:
Network And Affiliate Marketing

Chapter 7:
The Subconscious

Wrapping Up

Foreword

Unless you've found a way to live entirely free, you likely need some sort of steady income in order to endure. The traditional way to bring in revenue, naturally, is by having a job. You work for a company or begin your own, and the work you do earns you revenue, which you spend on things like a mortgage, rent, food, apparel, utilities and amusement.

Most individuals commonly work from their company's central location, a physical space where everybody from that organization gathers to exchange ideas and organize their efforts.

However, a few lucky souls have discovered ways to make revenue within the comfort of their own home. With the Net, an ever-changing arena for businesses, some looking to bring in revenue are discovering ways to do so.

A few forms are best for part-time endeavors for those looking to make a little extra revenue on the side, while other people may lead to full-time jobs and Net success stories. We've put together ways to make money on the Net, in no particular order.

Think And Grow Rich In The Knowledge Era
Practical Methods On Earning Big Money In The 21st Century.

Chapter 1:
Beginning With Content

Synopsis

If you are to bring in never-ending money, Blogging is a great choice. Quality content and writing style is the key to a great blog. Traffic and cash are by-products. So for a beginning you have to build a blog and write the things that you're great at.

If you're great at it, results will follow in about 3 month's time. Chief source of money for bloggers is advertisement like Google Adsense, Adbrite etc.

Blogs

Blogs can be for business or pleasure. A lot of individuals now earn part-time or even full-time earnings by blogging for cash.

Pick out a blog. There are free hosted blogs online through a lot of sources that may help you by giving you the tools and resources to make it easy to begin your own blog. Or you are able to register a domain name and begin your blog from scratch if you've a bit of technical smarts.

Pick out a niche. Once you've decided on a blog, determine what you'll write about to draw in visitors. A few simply utilize their blog as a place to write editorials or opinions while other people blog about a particular subject they're knowledgeable on. A lot of professional bloggers recommend that you pick out a niche so you are able to build a following.

Advertise your blog. Utilize web services that will get you some attention like blog directories and social bookmarking. Utilizing these services may help you get indexed in search engines and get traffic to your blog. Remarking on other blogs may likewise build links in to your blog and help more individuals find you. Once you've some material to read and are indexed in search engines, you are able to start to truly monetize your blog and start earning money.

Monetize

Sign on with Google Adsense. Google provides the ability for individuals to display targeted ads on their blog. Google will give you a part of that revenue when individuals: click on the ads, view the ads and buy something from a sponsor. You have to apply to Google Adsense and wait for acceptance, and then you'll have to work with your blog program to embed the code so the ads display right. This isn't hard.

You have to follow Google's TOS (terms of service) in order to sustain good standing.

Apply to other sites that pay you to post on your blog. There are a lot of blog sites that will pay you a flat fee for writing a particular ad and link into your blog. Sites like Payperpost, Blogitive or Blogvertise offer these services once your blog has been indexed in search engines like Google.

Apply for pro blogging jobs. A lot of web classified networks advertise the ability to post on your own blog or on a blog belonging to a company. A lot of freelance bloggers bring in a regular revenue by blogging this way.

Link up with affiliate programs like Amazon and Chikita Mini Malls that provide the ability to advertise on your blog. A lot of affiliate marketing programs exist that allow you to monetize your blog and bring in based on click through rates.

Maintain

Update your blog on a regular basis. By keeping your blog fresh, you draw in readers who will keep coming back and who may click your ads or purchase advertised services.

Append reader services to your blog like RSS (Really Simple Syndication) feeds to allow syndication and to draw in more readers. Continually discovering ways to grow and better your blog will better your money-earning potential.

Promote. Once you're bringing in cash from your blog, better your earning potential by paying for promoting in places that fit your niche. You are able to likewise accomplish this by trading links and banners with other pro bloggers to better exposure for your blog.

If you've a particular passion for something, whether it's a sideline or an obsession, and you've something to say about it, blogging could be a profitable way to spill out your endless stream of thought. The key here, as with a lot of other services on the Net, is in selling advertising.

After embarking on a personal blog, many writers sign up for ad services like Google AdSense, which post those familiar sponsored links you frequently see at the top and on the sides of sites. The more times your blog readers click on those ads, the more money you'll make through the ad service. This works fine if you're a nonchalant blogger, and you might make some extra spending money. But if the blog is consistently intriguing, well-written and really takes off, you might be approached by companies who wish to reach your fan base with graphical advertising around your blog. A few of the more successful blogs, like I Can Has Cheezburger? and Boing Boing, have gotten to be pop-culture phenomena, and their creators have been able to give up their day jobs and blog full time because of the cash they make from advertisers.

Chapter 2:
Auction Sites

Synopsis

It's a fairly aboveboard concept that most individuals are familiar with by now -- if you've a bunch of stuff that you don't necessarily need but other people want and are willing to pay exceedingly inflated prices for; you are able to auction off the items on eBay or other net auction sites. Simply gather your goods, produce a seller's profile and begin selling.

Ebay

Is it your dream to sit at home and bring in cash? Well, it's true for most of us. You'll be surprised at how easy it may be to make cash on eBay! It all just hinges upon what you wish to sell. Here are a few steps to get you started out:

Determine what you would like to sell. It may be electronics, apparel, toys, jewelry or items for which you've an interest.

Discover a wholesaler. You are able to look online for ones that have what you're looking for and who have excellent prices.

Sign on with the wholesaler. Commonly, all it takes is a free subscription to their site or newsletter. You then have access to all their prices and will know when they're having liquidation on particular items.

Buy a couple of items and place them for sale on eBay. You don't need to buy too many bulk items in case some things don't sell well.

Watch and explore eBay to see what are hot sellers. Purchase more of these items and place them for sale on the web site for those that are trading slowly, lower the prices.

Sell, sell, and sell! Try your best to distribute everything you have. This will give you a higher eBay seller rating. If you're having a difficult time selling an item, make it cheaper or add a bonus for a buy.

Make it your mission to sustain track of what's voguish, so that you are able to add it to your listings. This will keep purchasers coming back!

Your local Wal-Mart carries all sorts of items that are great sellers on eBay. You may be thinking, "Why would anybody purchase these items on eBay, when they may simply go to a Wal-Mart and buy them?" That's the point, perhaps they can't.

Wal-Mart isn't accessible to everybody in every corner of the world, nor do all Wal-Mart's carry the precise same merchandise. Learn what to buy at Wal-Mart to resell on eBay for revenue.

Part of the trick of selling Wal-Mart items is recognizing what eBay international site to list them. A few of the items below will sell best on a site other than eBay United States of America.

Have a look at the sports fan apparel for your local sports teams. I live in Phoenix. My local Wal-Mart is stocked with University of Arizona, Arizona State, Phoenix Suns, and Cardinal fan clothes. But, there are fans of these sports teams all over the globe who can't inevitably go to a Wal-Mart to buy them. Try selling football jerseys, hoodies, jackets, tee shirts, and flags. You are able to make some truly big profits selling fan apparel and accessories if a local team makes it to the playoffs.

Electronics. The huge one here is the Wii or whatever the latest and biggest video game system is. Purchase electronics prior to the holiday season and put them up for sale in mid-November. Likewise keep an eye on the popular Wii games - last year's blistering game was Guitar Hero. Check the eBay Pulse for what's blistering in the category of video games.

Walt Disney particulars. Last year, the rage was Hannah Montana and High School Musical, and a couple of years prior to that the rage was Lizzie McGuire. Touch base with the tween generation and discover what (and who) they're going nuts over. Hannah Montana bedding sets sold for three times the Wal-Mart shelf price as the items were so scarce, yet kids wanted them for Christmas Day and their parents were willing to pay.

Toy marketers on eBay make a killing during November and December but you have to have the flexibility and availability to go shopping at 2 AM to get the "red-hot toy" as soon as it's stocked. Pay attention to the hot Barbie particulars, Fisher Price toys (particularly electronic learning toys), LeapFrog/Leapster systems and games, and the latest Legs. Harry Potter sets do well. Playthings do exceptionally well year round on eBay UK, eBay Canada, and eBay Australia.

Action figures. Look for whatever the cutting-edge trend or popular movie hero is. Star Wars figures are forever popular, especially on eBay UK and eBay Europe.

Youngsters' digital cameras. The most popular camera is called the Fisher Price "Kid Tough" camera and is pink or blue. There's even a sub aquatic version. These sell at Wal-Mart for about $48.00. On eBay UK, they sell for about $85. Recoup your fees, and this item alone may bring about $30 in simply one sale. Just go to eBay UK, search the completed listings, and do your research before setting your beginning price.

Food. Individuals all over the world love our American junk food (even though it's obliterating us). In the UK, they need Lucky Charms. The Lucky Charms leprechaun holds a particular place in the hearts of the British and Irish. You are able to sell boxes of Lucky Charms for about three times the Wal-Mart price. They aren't purchasing the cereal for the taste; they're purchasing it because it's a novelty and they like the little leprechaun. Additional great selling food items include Oreos, M&Ms, Flaming Hot Cheetos, Tabasco, Hidden Valley Ranch powdered dressing mix, Kool-Aid powdered drink mix, BBQ sauces, Altoids mints, and gum.

Discontinued items. Cosmetics and skincare products are constantly being discontinued and these particulars may go for big cash on eBay. At one point in 2008, a $10 tube of Aveeno cream was selling for $40 as it had been discontinued.

Check your local Wal-Mart for particular regional foods. In Phoenix, our stores carry candy from Mexico, which are local favorites. Test market cities also have items that aren't found elsewhere. See what you are able to discover that's unique to your area.

It sounds easy, but takes some practice to sell successfully. Producing persuasive and legitimate product pages for the goods you're selling will help get purchasers interested. It's likewise crucial to set reasonable minimum bids to ensure that individuals will buy. And remember to deliver the sort of customer service that will garner positive feedback ratings and to communicate with purchasers to let them know you're reliable. The more positive feedback you get, the more individuals will be willing to do business with you. And that, naturally, means more money.

Chapter 3:
Transcription and Translation

Synopsis

Are you a fast typer? Do you speak a foreign language? Do you have a brain for legal or medical language? Welcome to the world of transcription and translation.

Translation jobs offer the better pay. Businesses, book publishers, sites -- just about anybody who produces marketing or editorial material -- need the help of experienced translators to push their products into fresh global markets.

In the medical field, hospitals and doctors offices require trained transcriptionists and coders to document procedures for insurance policy and record-keeping purposes. Law offices likewise need quick, accurate typers who may transcribe an audio or video of a deposition.

Type It

Get a medical transcription education. Employers will favor applicants who have some training in medical transcription. The Net has made it possible to get training and education in medical transcription without leaving your house. You may search for programs through a Net search engine.

There are many schools that provide education in medical transcription. You may visit the schools' sites and apply for admission to in medical transcription classes. You might have the option to enter a medical transcription completion certificate, associate's degree, or bachelor's degree. You'll be able to attend your classes on the Net and complete your education at home.

Sometime you complete your education; you'll have to search for a job. You might be aware of local medical offices that need medical transcriptionists. If not, searching the Net might be beneficial in discovering employment. Sites, such as Monster, Indeed and Careerbuilder are great places online to start you in your search in finding home-based jobs in medical transcription.

Find a company that provides transcribing jobs. To do so type into your browsers search box the words "transcription jobs". Many choices will come up in your search. Decide if you wish to transcribe medical or general audios and videos. If it's medical, you might need additional training and certification.

At this point you might have to sign up for a program to learn before you are able to earn. If it's non-medical, some companies online offer jobs for non-medical audio and video transcription.

Apply to the company that you would like to transcribe for. You might need to submit a resume while others just have a short application process.

Get equipment that you require. To be successful on the job, you'll need a PC, a printer, a fax capability, a copier, and a transcriber machine, as well as peculiar equipment to perform medical transcription.

You may buy a foot pedal, as well as voice recognition package to speed up the transcription process. Your employer might provide you with all the equipment you require. If not, you might buy this equipment at local office supply stores or from firms that sell them on the Net.

Set aside a particular time of the day to transcribe. Keeping this time of the day reserved only for transcribing will keep your job running smoothly. You are able to plan on working during these particularly designated hours.

Expect to get paid as much as you work. If you only work a bit, you'll only get paid a bit. If you work more, you'll get paid more. There's work out there for you as a transcriptionist. Once you discover a company that provides this type of work, you are able to start make money transcribing online.

If the Net has taught us anything, it's that business and revenue are no longer confined by borders. And anybody with a site and good marketing savvy may make millions of dollars online. There are booming markets in huge industrial markets like India and Japan with consumers who visit U.S. Sites daily for services and products. Because of global B2B transactions, a lot of these consumers have learned English to take full advantage of products and services offered by U.S. merchants and enterprisers. However, the majority of your potential niche demographic is still untapped, as your site may not be offered in their native language. Here are a few tips on how to translate your site to reach these potential customers.

The first method of translation I highly advocate is the utilization of translation scripts for sites or plugins for blogs. You may generally cut and paste the scripts into your web pages or download and install the plugins into your blogs.

The second technique involves utilizing a language translation tool for your site that typically translates English text into most other languages and vice versa. This is a manual process and not the best recommended. A few very popular and frequently utilized translation tools are offered by Google, Altavista, Babelfish, and Dictionary.com. You merely type or cut and paste your English text in a form and select the language you wish to translate your text to.

The third technique is hiring a translation firm that specializes in site translations, but make certain their software is compatible with the programming language of your site. They ought to be able to handle HTML, Cascading Style Sheets, and simple texts.

Search engine optimization is top priority for any site in any language, so include the appropriate foreign keywords in your page title, first paragraphs of each page, images, meta tags (keep to a minimum), and tag labels on your blogs.

Proofread and copy edit your work. Remember to tweak your site to the foreign audiences needs, and be careful and sensitive of word usage. You don't want to lose site visitors with a translation that comes across as offensive into any specific language.

Begin your own language translation business. A lot of services out there offer work to translators, but anybody with the translation skills may simply begin running a translation business from a home computer. Post a message advertising your services on forums and message boards online.

As you produce quality translation work, you'll find repeat buyers returning and recommending your services to others. Make sure to post ads for your services in all of the languages in which you're fluent, so you've the ability to reach potential customers regardless what the customer's native language may be.

Chapter 4:
Writing e-Books

Synopsis

Many individuals produce e-books with the intent to make cash. With that in mind you have to make certain you're offering your informative e-books in a way that will best benefit you and the consumer. Proper marketing of your books will give you the opportunity to make cash. Below are a few easy things you are able to do to make revenue from your e-books.

Become An Author

To make income from your e-books you'll first need to market your information. You are able to do this easily by allowing other publishers to utilize excerpts from your e-Book on their site or in their books. If somebody can get a glimpse of your info and find it useful, they'll be more willing to pay a fee to see what additional information they may get from your books to help them.

If you can't find great publishers for your write-up, you are able to make a PDF of it and sell it online on Amazon or eBay. If you've a blog, you are able to use that as a medium to sell it too. You simply have to provide an extract online. Users will then request an e-copy, if they like it. They can get it, when they have done the payment.

You are able to look into selling ad spaces. You are able to enhance your earnings on your e-book by sell ad space to different marketers who will compliment your e-book(s).

You are able to charge money for the ad to show on your books. This all depends on how much traffic you're getting to your e-book and how many you're selling. A few individuals can charge up to 500 dollars or more on truly successful e-books.

Sell your e-book for profit. This step is likely the fastest way to begin earning a solid income from your books. You are able to make a site and write helpful hints that will help you sell your e-book. Also, you are able to ask for testimonials from prior customers who bought them.

You ought to learn how to give a brief example of what will be in the book if you plan on selling it. This will make it easier for individuals to get interested in buying it and make you money.

You are able to likewise utilize back links in your e-book to get more traffic to your web site. More traffic will mean more cash for you on ad sells.

After you've sold the e-Book, you are able to make extra money by selling valuable monthly updates to the e-Book. If your subject is something that's ever changing or needs updates, this is a great way to keep the money coming in from your book.

Next, you ought to look into making your e-Book available for offline utilization. There are still many individuals out there that would prefer to have the data in a hard copy. They feel it's more credible it they may hold the information in their hand neatly held together with a book binding. If you prefer not to produce an actual book, you'll be able to also look into making an informational video or audio book. This will greatly increase your customer base for a very minimal investment.

Lastly, to make money from your e-Books you ought to reinvent them to work for other markets. Many e-books are very general; if you add a little info to these books or change a few details, they'll be useful to several large groups of buyers. After you have reinvented your book, you are able to begin the marketing process over again and make even more money from your books!

Chapter 5:
Search Engine Optimization

Synopsis

Every site on the Net needs traffic and the chief source of traffic is through Search Engines. Search Engine Optimization makes sites more search engine friendly and gives them more traffic. SEO requires some technical know-how and if you are able to find time to take some extra SEO classes, you are able to make a living out of it and use it to better your own sites.

Optimize

Utilizing SEO optimization, or simply search engine optimization, to make revenue online is essential to any site or for profit business. SEO is a way of utilizing keywords to your advantage so that search engines like Google will rank you higher in their searches.

Page rank on web sites like Google is crucial because if you're not on the front page, chances become very slim that anyone will click on your web site.

Just The Basics

First off, you'll have to decide on either a page title or an article title depending upon what you're currently working on. Both have the same chief principle. Hopefully you already know what your chief focus is on, topic wise, for your article or web-page. Regrettably, SEO still requires quite a bit of brainstorming.

The most powerful tool I know of that you are able to use at this point is Google's AdWords keyword tool which will leave you view the number of searches preformed and the cost per click (ad wise) of particular keywords on Google.

This is highly vital, so begin typing in title ideas and see what you are able to come up with. After you discover a few good titles, it's time to type them into Google and see the competition on those particular keywords. If you can't compete then try a few new keywords.

Now that you've your keywords all picked out it's time to lace them correctly throughout the article or site. Oh, and naturally, put them in the title of the page or article. You'll want to be placing the keywords in every paragraph as appropriate. Attempt to put the keywords in a density of about 6%, meaning that for every 100 words, 6 of them are keywords. This is the most vital stage of SEO at this level.

Google will take note of this and (hopefully) both correctly place you on the search engine searches and place the appropriate ads if you utilize AdWords.

In order to further better your SEO you'll have to move onto much more advanced techniques. Try looking up a few of the many great SEO books out there on the issue, or if you'd like to improve your Search Engine Optimization without all the research, attempt looking up SEO education.

As we stated Search engine optimization (SEO) is the art of increasing the ranking or a site, or individual pages on a site, on Google and other search engines.

For a lot of businesses, being number one in the listings for their market (or at least on the first page) may mean the difference between success and failure. When you begin an SEO business, being at the top of the rankings shows you're good at your job

Create your own site. Include your email address, phone number and fax number, if you have one. It's crucial that you provide these basic contact details, or your potential clients will give up when they attempt to contact you but fail. Add a blog to your site so you are able to discuss issues relating to SEO. Optimize every page, and each blog entry, for maximum exposure.

Produce a page on your site discussing your basic fee structure and what you are able to offer your customers. Don't price yourself out of the market, but don't sell yourself short either. Make it clear that you're willing to structure your prices to your customers needs, depending upon the complexity of the job they have for you.

Advertise on an assortment of sites, and in the business pages of papers. When advertising online, the "cost per click" model is frequently the most cost effective, as your buyers will only pay for those individuals who view their sites.

Make your advert catchy but not over the top, and have it link to a particular page on your site that discusses why the reader ought to choose you for his SEO needs.

Chapter 6:
Network And Affiliate Marketing

Synopsis

You've decided that you wish to look into what everybody is talking about and get into network marketing.

Where do you begin? First, you have to find the business that you'll find interesting and you'll want to stick with. Researching yourself before you begin looking at companies. This will help you in your search.

- Do you like to help individuals? If so, how?
- What are your interests, likes, dislikes?
- What preceding experience do you have that may help.
- What type of matters are you interested in?

Begin looking around for Network marketing companies. It won't take long to find companies that are looking for you to join their team. In some cases, they may find you. You are able to go to many of the work at home portals and various job sites; simply type in "work at home" or "home business" and you'll find many. There are many sites that specialize in providing this sort of info to you through advertisements and message board entries that tell you what they do. Now you have looked around and chosen a few companies you wish to look into. What type of questions should you ask?

Finding A Company

- How long has the company been around?
- What will I be doing?
- What education is involved?
- Will I have a mentor/sponsor to assist me after the training?
- How long have you been with the company?
- How much will I be compensated?
- How long does it take before I begin seeing results?
- How will I be compensated?
- How much will it take for me to get moving?
- Are there any monthly/annual fees involved?

A few of these questions might seem kind of blunt, however these are crucial for you to know before you make a decision about a network marketing business. Don't agree to join till after you've had a chance to research the company. Give yourself a couple of days and set an appointment for them to call you back.

No matter what company it is, you ought to be able to research it. Check with the Better Business Bureau- there are ways to check net companies also.

Go to the work at home sites, and look for bulletin boards and forums. Join and begin asking questions. You may wish to ask the same questions everywhere to see if you get the same responses. It's good to talk to more than one person inside a company; this gives you a view from a different prospective.

They may have different techniques they utilization to be successful- and simply because one person is successful it doesn't mean

everybody will be, and vice versa. Go to the company's main site and look around.

Make a list with every company of the pros and cons that you have determined in your research and from talking to individuals with each company. There are a few crucial things to keep in mind when deciding. Regardless how good the company is if you're not willing to work and be trainable you will not succeed.

You have to go with a company that provides unlimited support or you'll find yourself with questions that you can't get answered. You'll be responsible for your own success in a lot of ways. You must train your downline.

In most cases with Network marketing your success is dependant on your downlines' success. For instance: To move up to the next level, your downline has to enroll and sign up a particular amount of business for you to promote.

This may be frustrating at times but may be overcome with a good training system in place that includes proven multiple ways to generate results. If you would rather be sitting on the couch viewing soap operas and eating Bon-bons, this business isn't for you.

You need to have an out-going, enthusiastic personality. You are able to get over being shy, but you must be comfortable speaking to individuals whether it is on the telephone or in person, depending upon the business.

You have to believe in what you're doing to be successful at it, and in order for you to have the motivation to pick up the telephone or to

speak to somebody about it. If you don't believe it is real then it won't be. When you find that company that you are able to stand behind, treat it as if it was yours, because after all- it is. If you just opened a coffeehouse, you'd believe that your coffee was the greatest right? Same attitude applies here. There aren't any "I will try it's" in this business. You have to be an "I will accomplish it" type individual to survive and succeed in network marketing.... This brings us to our next chapter.

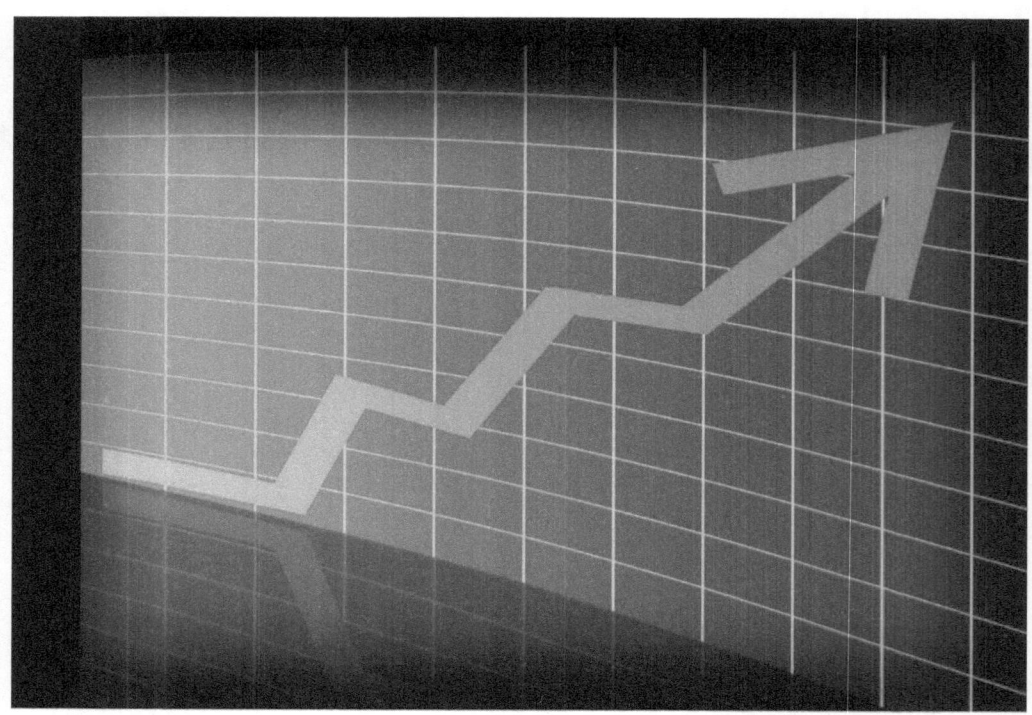

Chapter 7:
The Subconscious

Synopsis

Among the most important tings in becoming financially successful is the subconscious mind. The study of the subconscious is amazing, however, just to give you a little insight on what this part of the mind does... Your subconscious ties your shoes. Your subconscious drives your auto.

Do you consider doing these activities or do you just accomplish them? Have you ever heard of the term second nature? What makes a Jordan among the best basketball players that ever played? Michael spent hours upon hours practicing particular moves, shooting jumpers, and free throws.

This habit later would shift into an automatic response in the mind. It commonly takes about twenty-one days to break or make a habit, and then it becomes automatic.

Get Your Brain Right

As everything in our universe, including the thoughts that we think exist as a vibration resulting in a projection of complete energy, and those thoughts are first passed through and examined by the conscious mind before a belief may be established and stored, you've the choice and power to become consciously aware of and control what thoughts or data you let be recorded and stored.

You likewise have the option and power to alter or overwrite the existing data stored in the subconscious that you currently perceive as your truth or reality when you find that this data is contrary to or counterproductive to producing desired outcomes that you have a want to experience.

This may only be achieved by expanding your awareness...absorbing fresh data and establishing new beliefs based on the new data that's obtained.

This may only be accomplished by gathering fresh information or data from other sources that extend beyond where you obtained the original data expanding your awareness to new potential and/or possibilities outside of your currently "sensed comfort zone."

So how may you know if the data that you currently perceive as truth is limiting?

Look around you and note the quality of your life currently. Consider and become consciously aware of what you're thinking and feeling and you'll understand what you're attracting into your life right now.

If you're not living the life that you want, and are not experiencing peace, harmony, abundance, and joy in each aspect of your life, you require fresh information!

You don't require it in the literal sense of the word but to experience better results it will be essential to enhance and elevate the quality of the data.

So how do you get this fresh information? The first action necessary is to learn to get consciously aware of the continuous babbling which runs like a tape loop inside your conscious mind. This "apparently uncontrollable" babble points to what's been recorded and stored at a subconscious level.

The next step is become keenly and consciously aware of the quality of those consistent thought patterns.

Start asking yourself...why do you believe what you believe? Where did those notions come from? Are they real or only a limited "perception of truth?"

The following step is to become keenly and consciously cognizant of what you surround yourself with. What are you letting penetrate and be stored in your subconscious? What do you consistently expose yourself to in the physical world? Is it information that supports what you wish? Does it conflict with what you wish? When you become "witting and aware" of that you are able to start adjusting if necessary.

The last step is to become cognizant of and change the repetitive thoughts that aren't in alignment with what you want to experience.

The procedure, although it does take some discipline at first, is super simple, unbelievably potent and if consistently used and applied will start to produce results in your life that you might have previously "perceived" to be unachievable!

With practice, and by getting keenly aware of what your predominant thoughts consist of, and what you're letting into your mind, you are able to then take conscious control over what is given to and stored in your subconscious as truth. By doing this, your subconscious is limited to absorbing and storing only the consciously filtered data provided to it by the conscious mind.

If your thoughts and beliefs are in alignment with your desired outcome, the vibrations emitted and broadcast as a result of the emotions experienced are sent out into the cosmos (the field) and may only draw in like or harmonious vibrations or frequencies of the same favorable vibration, and produce in your physical reality those things that you want.

Wrapping Up

Growth is a process and life is a journey. The selections you make today, will and do, without question, determine the kind and quality of your results and experiences in the future. If the results that you've experienced thus far in your life haven't produced the results that you desire, it's obvious that fresh choices need to be made. Choose wisely.

Online jobs have the benefits of comfort of house and flexible schedules. Unlike office jobs, they have almost countless earning potential. If you know how to play it safe and do things in style, you'll earn big. Don't worry; you'll learn to utilize your own style. Now begin working.

Good Luck!